Golf 101

with Bob Dimpleton™

"Essential Information for the Junior or Beginner Golfer."

Written & Illustrated

by

Mark G. Kuhn
Head Golf Professional

Published by the Auth

*This book is dedicated
to all my family and friends who have
supported and motivated me over the years.
Thank you!!!*

**Grateful acknowledgement to Warwick Massey for providing the
Bob Dimpleton name.
Hot air balloon photo courtesy of Fantasy Balloon Charters**

Library and Archives Canada Cataloguing in Publication
Kuhn, Mark G., 1965-
Golf 101 with Bob Dimpleton : essential information for the junior
or beginner golfer / written and illustrated by Mark G. Kuhn
ISBN: 978-0-9737517-0-3
1. Golf. I. Title
GV965.K84 2005   796.352   C2005-901132-7

Published by Mark G. Kuhn
Website address: www.bobdimpleton.com

Printed in Hong Kong

This book is designed for the young golfer of any age. Master Golf Instructor, Bob Dimpleton, will guide and teach you golf's essentials. Sit back and enjoy your journey. Bob is the BEST!!!

Table of Contents

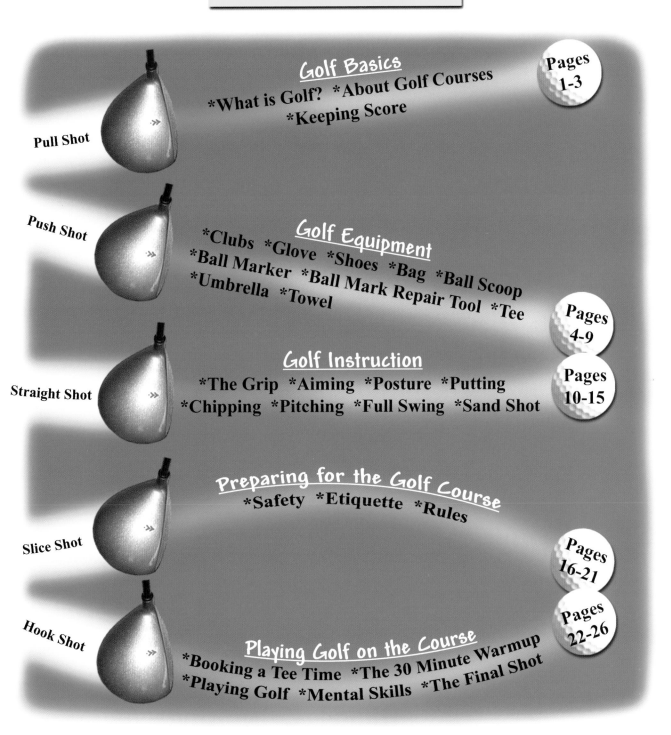

Golf Basics

What is golf?

Golf is a sport played on a big area of grass called a golf course. The objective of golf is to hit a golf ball into a hole with specially designed clubs. To play golf, tee up your ball on the #1 tee box and hit your ball   towards the #1   green.

On the #1 green you will find a hole with a flag in it. The number of times you hit the ball to get it into the hole from the tee box is your score on #1. Write that score on your scorecard. Then proceed to the 2nd tee box and play that hole.

Par	3	3	3	3	3	3	3	3	3	27		3	3	3	3	3	3	3	3	3	27	54
Yardage	124	105	107	96	86	82	92	74	147	913		138	97	84	117	86	63	81	94	161	921	1834
Hole #	1	2	3	4	5	6	7	8	9	OUT		10	11	12	13	14	15	16	17	18	IN	Total
CATHY	4	3	5	2	4	6	4	3	2	33		4	3	4	2	5	3	4	3	5	33	66
JEREMY	5	3	4	3	3	5	2	3	4	32		2	3	3	4	4	3	2	5	4	30	62
DAVE	6	4	5	2	3	3	4	6	4	37		6	4	3	5	5	4	3	4	5	39	76

After you finish playing all the holes on the golf course (usually 9 or 18), add up your score on each hole and that is your total score for the day.

About Golf Courses

Golf courses generally come in small, medium or large sizes. Small golf courses only have Par 3 holes. Medium size golf courses have Par 3 and Par 4 holes and large golf courses have Par 3, Par 4, and Par 5 holes.

Be Creative!!! Try drawing your own golf holes.

A par 3 hole generally ranges from 50 to 200 or more yards from the tee box to the green. On a Par 3, you should try to land your ball on the green in one shot.

A par 4 hole generally ranges from 200 to 450 or more yards from the tee box to the green. On a Par 4, you should try to hit your ball onto the fairway before your next shot onto the green. If you miss the fairway, your next shot will be more challenging.

A Par 5 hole generally ranges from 400 to 600 or more yards from the tee box to the green. Because Par 5's are the longest holes, it will require 2, 3, 4 or more shots to reach the green.

Keeping Score

In keeping score, a shot is counted every time you hit or try to hit the golf ball with any club in your golf bag. If you swing and miss the ball while trying to hit it, that is considered 1 shot. However if you practice swing, that is not a shot.

The small golf course scorecard

Par	3	3	3	3	3	3	3	3	3	27		3	3	3	3	3	3	3	3	3	27	54
Yardage	124	105	107	96	86	82	92	74	147	913		138	97	84	117	86	63	81	94	161	921	1834
Hole #	1	2	3	4	5	6	7	8	9	OUT		10	11	12	13	14	15	16	17	18	IN	Total
TYLER	4	3	2	3	5	4	3	3	2	29		2	3	3	3	4	2	3	3	6	29	58
BREAH	2	5	6	4	3	3	4	6	2	35		3	1	5	2	2	3	4	4	3	27	62

The Large golf course scorecard

White tee yardage	519	365	195	369	386	123	345	500	397	3199		371	345	453	330	149	377	254	139	467	2885	6084
Red tee yardage	443	315	167	315	337	107	308	440	355	2787		308	306	409	311	127	322	214	103	426	2526	5313
Hole #	1	2	3	4	5	6	7	8	9	OUT		10	11	12	13	14	15	16	17	18	IN	Total
GREG	5	4	3	5	6	2	4	7	4	40		6	4	7	4	4	5	5	3	8	46	86
JANET	6	3	3	4	4	3	5	3	4	35		4	3	5	6	3	4	3	4	4	36	71
Par	5	4	3	4	4	3	4	5	4	36		4	4	5	4	3	4	4	3	5	36	72

The best golfers in the world shoot under par on a regular basis and some golfers have even shot a 59 on a par 72 which is -13 under par for the course. WWOOOW!!! It doesn't get much better than that.

Golf Equipment

Can you find all the golf equipment in the picture?

* Golf Clubs
* Golf Hat
* Golf Glove
* Golf Shoes
* Golf Bag
* Ball Scoop
* Ball Marker
* Ball Mark Repair Tool
* Golf Tee
* Golf Ball
* Umbrella
* Towel

Golf Clubs

A set of golf clubs consists of woods, irons and a putter. Each club is designed to hit a golf ball a different distance. To determine how far you hit each of your clubs, refer to the Bob Dimpleton scale of distances below. Go to a practice facility and find out how many yards you hit your 7 iron. Then find the scale that most closely matches to your 7 iron distance. This scale will estimate how far you hit some of your other clubs.

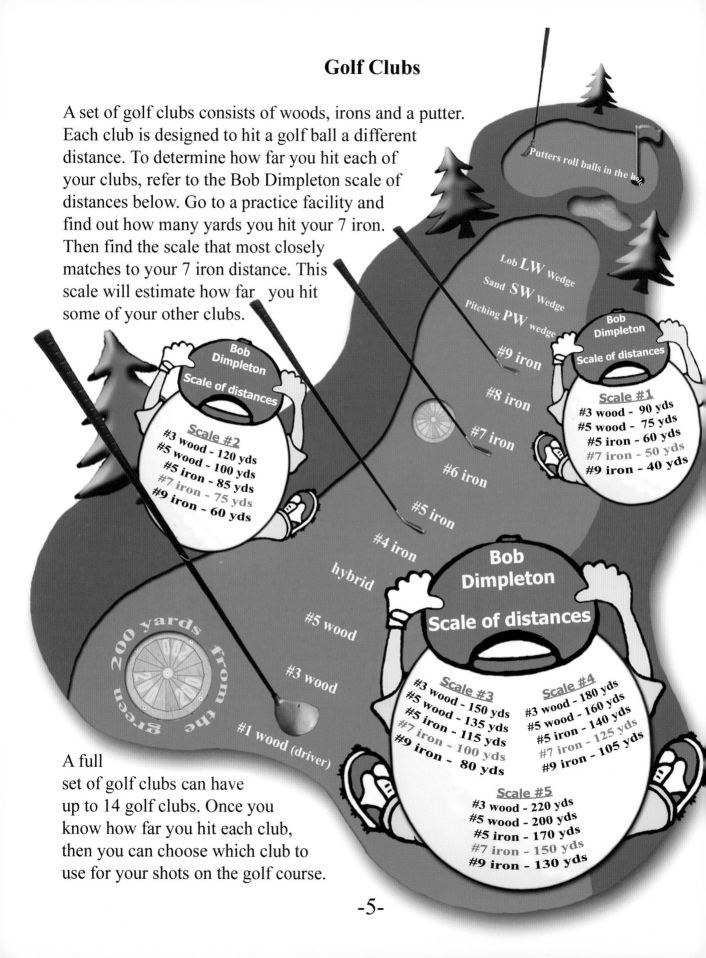

Putters roll balls in the hole

Lob **LW** Wedge
Sand **SW** Wedge
Pitching **PW** wedge

#9 iron

#8 iron

#7 iron

#6 iron

#5 iron

#4 iron

hybrid

#5 wood

#3 wood

#1 wood (driver)

200 yards from the green

Bob Dimpleton
Scale of distances

Scale #1
#3 wood - 90 yds
#5 wood - 75 yds
#5 iron - 60 yds
#7 iron - 50 yds
#9 iron - 40 yds

Bob Dimpleton
Scale of distances

Scale #2
#3 wood - 120 yds
#5 wood - 100 yds
#5 iron - 85 yds
#7 iron - 75 yds
#9 iron - 60 yds

Bob Dimpleton
Scale of distances

Scale #3
#3 wood - 150 yds
#5 wood - 135 yds
#5 iron - 115 yds
#7 iron - 100 yds
#9 iron - 80 yds

Scale #4
#3 wood - 180 yds
#5 wood - 160 yds
#5 iron - 140 yds
#7 iron - 125 yds
#9 iron - 105 yds

Scale #5
#3 wood - 220 yds
#5 wood - 200 yds
#5 iron - 170 yds
#7 iron - 150 yds
#9 iron - 130 yds

A full set of golf clubs can have up to 14 golf clubs. Once you know how far you hit each club, then you can choose which club to use for your shots on the golf course.

Before you buy golf clubs, it is a good idea to take some golf lessons from your local P.G.A. golf professional. If you then decide to buy clubs, ask your pro about custom club fitting. Custom club fitting makes sure that the clubs that you buy, fit your body type and swing. There are a number of tests a club fitter will do.

Lie Angle Test

Toe is up too much
(Ball will go left)

Bottom edge is level
(Ball will go straight)

Toe is down too much
(Ball will go right)

This test is done while hitting balls

Grip thickness test!!!

One test will help you find clubs with the proper lie angles. One test will make sure that the thickness of your grips are right. Other tests will make sure that each club's shaft fits you. Your local P.G.A. pro can conduct these tests or help you find a club fitter that can.

Too Small

Too Big

Too Big

Bob Dimpleton

Not only should your golf clubs fit you, but your other equipment should fit you as well.

The Glove

Wearing a glove helps prevent your club from slipping. Right handed golfers should wear a snug fitting glove on their left hand. Their right hand doesn't require a glove.

Golf Shoes

Golf shoes help prevent your feet from slipping. They also stabilize your feet better than most other footwear. If you do not have golf shoes, golf courses will allow you to wear sneakers or running shoes.

The Golf Bag

The golf bag is needed to carry your golf clubs, balls, tees or anything you feel you may need on a golf course such as food, drink, umbrella, ball scoop or raingear, etc. You can choose to carry your golf bag on your shoulders or push your bag on a cart.

I like to carry my clubs.

I find it easier to push my clubs on a cart.

The Ball Scoop

The ball scoop helps you retrieve your ball from tough to reach places. Here Bob is scooping his ball out of the creek.

The Ball Marker

When your ball comes to rest on a putting green, you are allowed to mark and lift your golf ball. Here's how you do this.

Place a ball marker or coin behind your ball, in line with the hole

and then pick your ball up.

By marking your golf ball, it will avoid distracting other golfers who putt before you and it allows you to clean your golf ball before you putt. When it is your turn to putt, just reverse the above process to return your ball to its original position.

The Ball Mark Repair Tool

2 thumbs up for everyone who marks their ball and fixes their ball mark!

Bob Dimpleton

Whenever your ball lands on the green, it creates a hole in the ground called a ball mark. Use a ball mark repair tool or a tee to repair this hole. Here's how.

Pry the hole up with your

ball mark repair tool and then

tap the ground with your putter.

If everyone fixes their own ball marks, the greens will always be smooth to putt on!!!

The Tee

A tee is used to prop your golf ball up when you are hitting shots off of the tee box. The only time you're allowed to tee your ball up is the 1st shot on each hole.

Tee up the ball for the 3 wood, 5 wood and all the irons approximately half an inch.

Tee up the ball for a #1 wood (driver) approximately an inch and a half.

If you need to adjust these tee heights, just pull or push the tee up or down in the ground.

The Umbrella

Bob Dimpleton

Other than rain, some players use an umbrella to protect themselves from the sun.

The Towel

The towel clips onto your golf bag and is used to clean your equipment as you play your round of golf.

Golf Instruction

The Grip 101

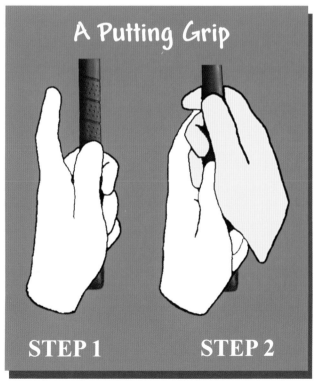

A Putting Grip

STEP 1   STEP 2

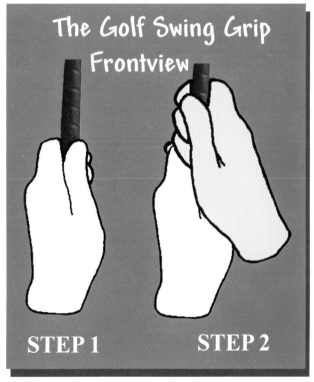

The Golf Swing Grip
Frontview

STEP 1   STEP 2

Aiming 101

Posture 101

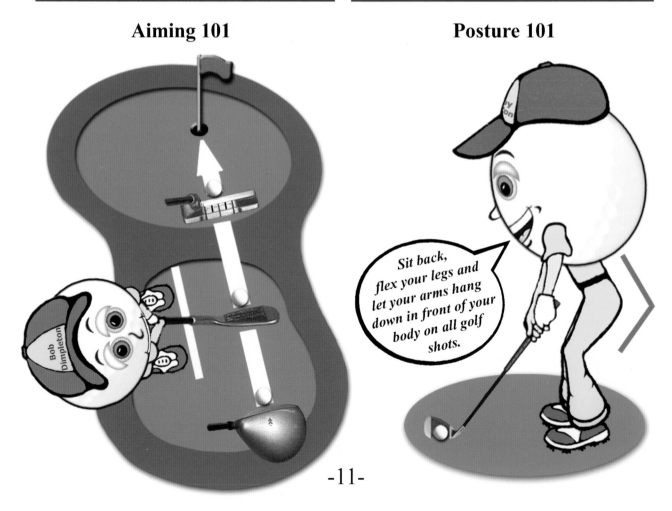

-11-

Putting 101

Putting is chosen when your ball is on the putting green. You use your putter to roll the ball along the ground and into the hole.

To putt, position yourself like Bobby Dimpleton. Copy his ball position, eye position, posture, grip and feet placement (stance). Then, make a pendulum-like motion with your club, arms and shoulders while keeping your head and legs still.

This is a good way to putt, but maybe you can discover a better way to putt. You might like a different putting grip or a different stance width. As with all the golf instruction in this book, you should still experiment and learn new ideas from your local P.G.A. golf professional, golf books or magazines. Then go out and Practice!!!

Practice!!!   Practice!!!   Practice!!!

Chipping 101

Putting is chosen when your ball is on the putting green, but chipping is chosen when your ball is close to the putting green (usually within 5 yards). It is a low shot that travels through the air, lands on the green and then rolls to the hole.

Practice chipping with a 9 iron first. As you improve, experiment chipping with other irons or woods. Then you can decide which club suits you the best.

To chip, look at Bobby Dimpleton's setup. Copy his starting ball position, stance, posture and grip. Notice that he begins with a little more weight on his left foot and his hands begin in a position in front of the ball. Once you have this setup, take a pendulum-like motion similar to that of putting.

Golf Swing 101

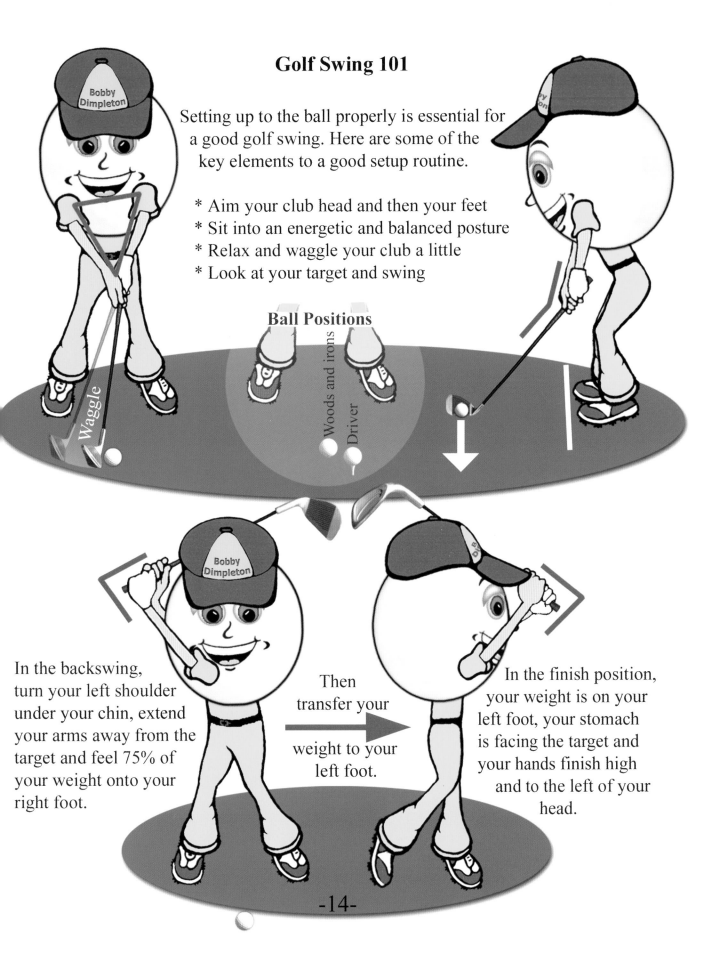

Setting up to the ball properly is essential for a good golf swing. Here are some of the key elements to a good setup routine.

* Aim your club head and then your feet
* Sit into an energetic and balanced posture
* Relax and waggle your club a little
* Look at your target and swing

Ball Positions

Woods and irons

Driver

Waggle

In the backswing, turn your left shoulder under your chin, extend your arms away from the target and feel 75% of your weight onto your right foot.

Then transfer your weight to your left foot.

In the finish position, your weight is on your left foot, your stomach is facing the target and your hands finish high and to the left of your head.

The golf swing ideas that you learned on the previous page can be used for all of your full swings with woods or irons. If you are a left handed golfer, look at the pictures in this book through a mirror and then you will see Bobby as a left handed golfer. Practice Bobby's setup, backswing and finish positions. When you hit balls, develop a smooth, flowing motion from the setup, through the backswing and into the finish position. This smooth, flowing motion will help you to repeat your golf swing with consistency.

For shots that are 5 to 50 yards from the green, use your shortest hitting iron, shorten your backswing, and play the ball in the middle of your feet. This is called a pitch shot and is used when you are too far from the green to chip but too close to the green to take a full swing. The picture shows you estimated areas to use each shot that Bobby has shown you.

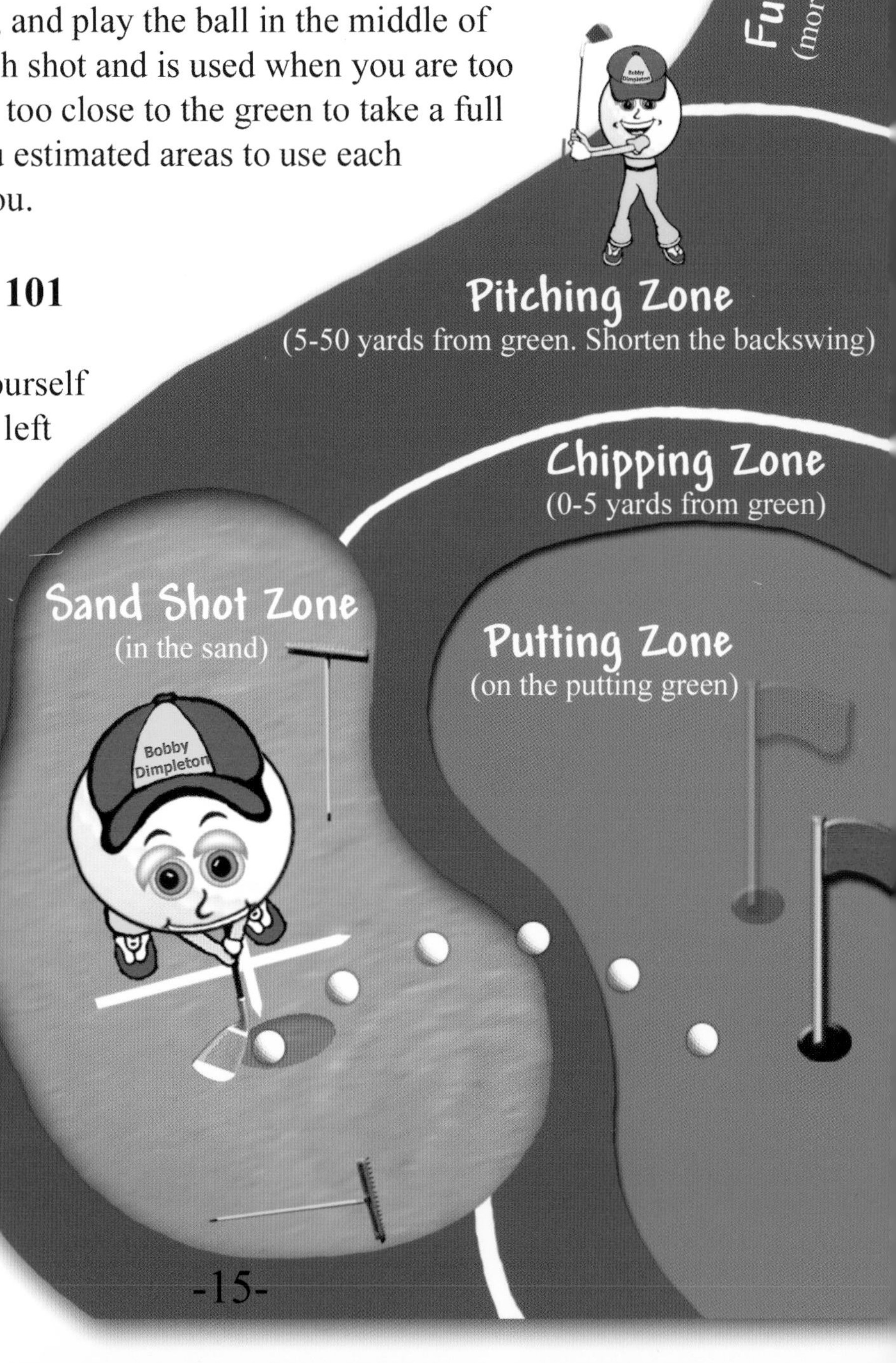

Full Swing Zone
(more than 50 yards)

Pitching Zone
(5-50 yards from green. Shorten the backswing)

Greenside Sand Shot 101

To play this sand shot, aim yourself to a pretend flag that is to the left of the real flag. Then turn the clubface of your sand wedge so it aims to the right.

When you take your swing, splash an oval of sand out from under the ball as highlighted in the picture.

Your sand wedge never touches the ball. The sand you splash propels the ball out.

Follow through on this shot.

Chipping Zone
(0-5 yards from green)

Sand Shot Zone
(in the sand)

Bobby Dimpleton

Putting Zone
(on the putting green)

Preparing for the Golf Course

Safety 101

The 1st priority in golf is safety. IT'S IMPORTANT TO BE AWARE of what dangers lie on a golf course. The club and the ball can hurt you and so can a golf course with its deep water hazards or unlevel ground.

A golf club is made up of very hard materials that travel very fast when a golfer swings it. To avoid injury from a club, there are 3 rules.

RULE #1 - do not throw your club
RULE #2 - do not get closer than 5 yards to a person swinging a club
RULE #3 - do not swing if someone is closer than 5 yards from you

The fence needs to be big enough so that if you swing, there is no chance of hitting someone with your club. Close your eyes right now and see if you can imagine a big white fence around you.

To prevent getting hurt from the golf ball you should never stand in front of a golfer hitting their shot. The black line below shows you this boundary. It's okay to stand behind the black line but if you stand in front of   the black line, you could get hit with the ball. Another way to get hit with   a golf ball is from a group of golfers playing a different hole. Whenever possible, be aware of the shots being made by other groups on the course.

If you accidentally hit your ball towards another group, yell "FORE!!!" as loud as you can in their direction. This warns them that your ball could hit them and that they should turn around and duck their heads.

Practice yelling "FORE!!!" really loud, like Bob Dimpleton.

Still other dangers on a golf course could come from holes or unlevel ground. Always watch where you are walking and obey all danger signs. Bob Dimpleton didn't obey the sign and look what's happening to him. To reduce your chance of slipping, always replace any worn out spikes on the bottom of your golf shoes.

Etiquette 101

Etiquette in golf is how you behave and conduct yourself on the golf course. Good etiquette makes golf fun for everyone. It includes taking care of the golf course, playing at a good pace, and respecting your playing partners.

To take care of the golf course, it is  important to repair your divots, repair your ball marks, rake the sand traps, and avoid placing equipment on, or near, the tee boxes or putting greens.

Repairing Divots

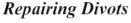

A divot is a piece of ground that gets taken out as you hit your shot. It is important to replace that divot back into its original spot or to fill the hole with a sand and seed mixture provided by the golf course. Doing this will repair the divot hole properly.

Raking Sand Traps

After taking your shot from the sand, you should rake your footprints level with the rakes provided by the golf course. This makes the course play fair for everyone. Can you find the rakes in the picture?

Placing Equipment

Golf bags and pull carts should stay off of the putting greens and tee boxes to prevent damaging the grass. Please take care of the golf course.

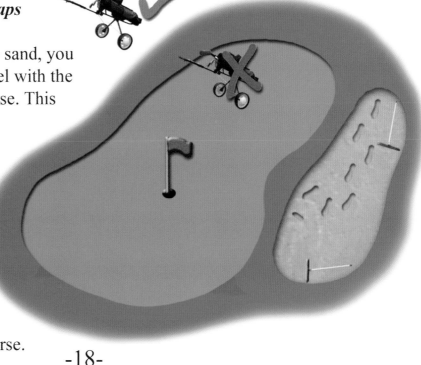

Pace of Play

A good pace of play for 4 players is approximately 3 3/4 to 4 1/4 hours for an 18 hole large golf course. An 18 hole small course should take approximately 2 - 2 1/4 hours to play.

To establish a good pace of play, note the time when you begin playing a hole and note the time when you finish playing a hole. Adjust your pace to match the Bob Dimpleton pace of play clocks. Because the smaller courses generally have shorter Par 3's than the larger golf courses, you should play those Par 3's in 7-8 minutes.

Respecting your Playing Partners

To respect your playing partners it is good etiquette to stand still and be quiet when they are hitting. Also, when you are on the putting green, try to avoid walking on their putting line as this could affect the true roll of their putt. Putting lines are shown as white lines in the picture below.

Encourage your playing partners.

Enjoy your time with them on the golf course.

This is good etiquette.

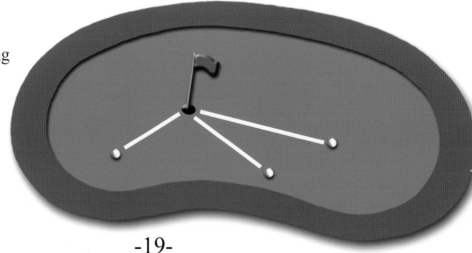

Golf Rules 101

There are 34 rules in the game of golf. At age 10, you should begin learning them. As you read the rule book, you will notice that the lakes and creeks are called water hazards or lateral water hazards. You will also come across terms such as out of bounds and bunker. The golf hole to the right shows you how to identify these parts on your golf course.

A water hazard is surrounded by yellow stakes in the ground, a lateral water hazard is surrounded by red stakes in the ground and out of bounds is identified by white stakes in the ground. The lines connecting to the stakes might be drawn on your golf course with paint or you will simply have to imagine them as straight lines in between the stakes.

In either type of water hazard, your ball is considered in the hazard if the whole ball is inside the colored lines or even if just a part of the ball touches the line.

Bunker

The rule book calls the sand a bunker

Water Hazard

Bob Dimpleton

Playing by the rules will give you your true score.

Lateral Water Hazard

Out of Bounds

On this hole, a ball is considered out of bounds if the whole ball is on the white line or to the right of the white line. A ball partly left of the white line is not considered out of bounds.

If your course doesn't have white stakes, then out of bounds is anywhere off of the golf course such as a neighbour's field, a highway or over the course's boundary fence.

The rules of golf say that if you hit a ball out of bounds, you have to hit another ball from the same place and add 2 to your score (stroke & distance). This means if your 1st shot goes out of bounds, you have to play another ball from the tee box as your 3rd shot.

If your ball rests in a water hazard or lateral water hazard, you can play the ball without a penalty. However, you can't let your club touch the ground before your shot or you get a 2 stroke penalty. Only play your ball from a water hazard if it is safe to do so and you believe you can hit a good shot.

Most times you will have to take a 1 stroke penalty and drop a new ball in a proper area.

A proper area is within 2 club lengths, not closer to the hole from the point your original ball flew over the hazard line and into the water.

The proper way to drop a ball is from shoulder height.

The tees in the picture to the left represent those original points and the shadows represent the 2 club length area that you are allowed to drop a new ball onto.

This is just 1 proper area for each hazard that you can drop a new ball. To discover the other proper areas you can drop a ball, read Rule 26 in the rule book.

The Bunker

The bunker is also considered a hazard. If your ball comes to rest in a bunker, avoid touching your club in the sand before your shot or you will get a 2 stroke penalty. However, there is no penalty for touching the sand with your club during the forward motion of your sand shot stroke.

Hover the club head above the sand before your shot

Playing golf on the course

Booking a Tee Time

The 1st step in playing golf on the course is making a reservation at the golf course. Bob is calling the golf shop to book a tee time for himself, his son Bobby and his daughter Betty. The course he is playing allows him to book groups of 2, 3 or 4 players by phone or online.

Hello, Can I book for 3 people for around 11:00am?

If Bob books for 2 players, the golf course may join another 2 players with him to make a foursome. However, since Bob has 3 players, the course will only allow 1 extra player to join his group.

To play alone as a group of 2 or 3, you would have to play when the golf course is not busy. Just ask the golf shop staff when those times are.

The 30 Minute Warmup

Once you have made your reservation, plan to arrive at the golf course 40 minutes or more before your tee time. When you arrive, find the golf shop and pay your green fee. Pick up a scorecard and pencil and begin the following warmup.

* 10 minutes practicing short, medium and long putts on the practice putting green

Hi, I'm Betty Dimpleton.

Next, spend 20 minutes warming up at the driving range. A driving range is a practice area where you can hit golf balls to develop your swing or warmup before your round of golf. To warmup, begin with at least 10 chip shots, 10 pitch shots and then some full swings. DO NOT SWING TOO HARD!!! Begin your full swings with your shortest irons and develop a consistent and smooth swing pace for the day.

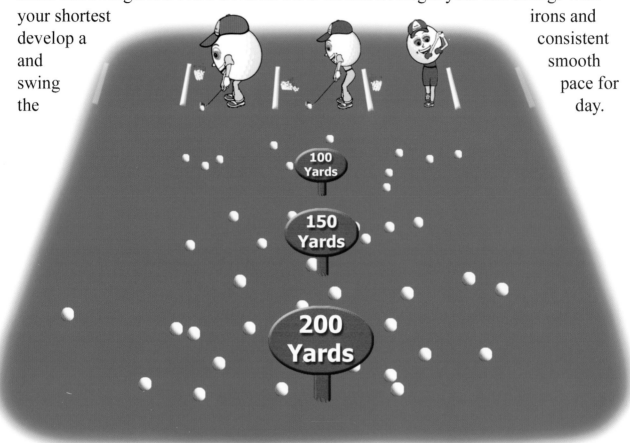

If the golf course you are going to does not have a driving range, then do the following 20 minute warmup routine at home before going to the course.

Take 5 full practice swings with a 9 iron, swinging slower than normal. Next, develop a good setup. Check your grip, aim, posture and ball position as Bobby Dimpleton instructed. You might need a mirror to check this. Once you have a good setup, then take a full backswing and hold that position for 5 seconds. Then go to your full finish position and hold that for 5 seconds. Take a rest and repeat the above routine with all your odd numbered clubs once or twice. After 20 minutes, you will be warmed up to play golf.

Warming up helps you to prevent injury and it also gets you mentally and physically ready to play golf.

Playing Golf

After your warmup, walk to the 1st tee box to prepare for your round of golf. The 1st tee box will have a sign beside it, indicating such things as how many yards the 1st hole is and what par it is. Your 1st decision is to determine what color tee markers to play from. If you choose to play from the red tee markers, you need to play from them on every hole. The same goes if you choose to play from the white tee markers or the blue tee markers. The white highlighted areas on the tee box indicate the proper area that you can tee up your ball for each set of tee markers.

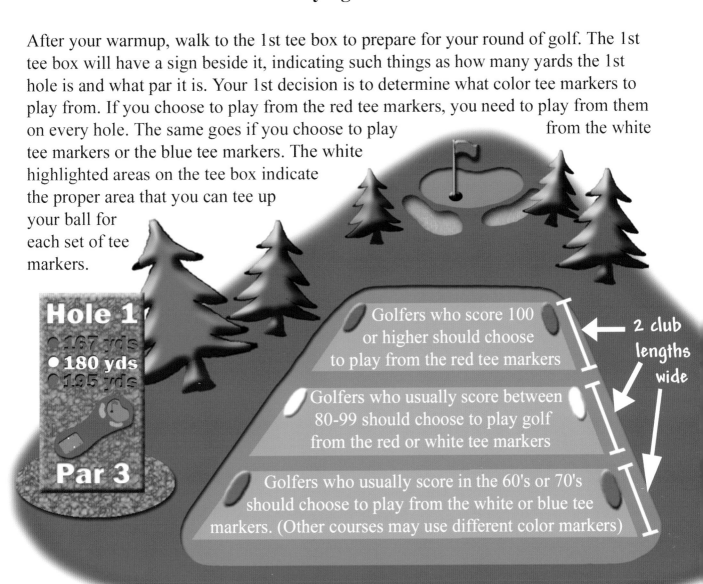

Hole 1
167 yds
● 180 yds
195 yds
Par 3

Golfers who score 100 or higher should choose to play from the red tee markers

2 club lengths wide

Golfers who usually score between 80-99 should choose to play golf from the red or white tee markers

Golfers who usually score in the 60's or 70's should choose to play from the white or blue tee markers. (Other courses may use different color markers)

Your 2nd decision is to choose which club you are going to use. Refer to the Bob Dimpleton Scale of distances to help you with this decision and then tee off. After everyone has hit their 1st shot, the farthest ball from the hole goes next. Play in this order until everyone gets their ball in the hole.

On the following holes, the person with the lowest score from the previous hole, tees off 1st. This is called "having the honor." The 2nd lowest score tees off 2nd and so on and so on until everyone hits. If scores were tied, then always tee off in the same order as the previous hole.

Mental Skills 101

In preparation for each shot on the course, there are proven methods that can improve how you play. Yes, eating right, exercising properly and getting plenty of rest can improve your performance but what about thinking right? Thinking positively has always been at the core of all successful athletes. Are you a person who generally thinks more positively or more negatively?

If you believe that you are more of a negative thinker, then begin with positive self talk. Tell yourself that you are better than you really are in order to become better than you really are. Eliminate all self talk that begins with the words "I can't", such as, "I can't putt" or "I can't hit anything today." This is negative self talk that can zap the energy you need to play your best.

Next, try getting into a routine of imagining your best shot before every shot. Stand behind your ball and picture it flying to your target or in the case of putting, picture your ball rolling into the middle of the hole. The best results generally come from those people who work hard, with positive images running through their mind.

Finally, when you are waggling the club before your swing, look at your target a couple of times and then swing. You now have the best chance of playing your best. Thinking like this, along with lessons from your local P.G.A. professional, will change your game. Believe it and you can achieve it.

The Final Shot

Putting is generally the last shot you make on a golf hole. Before you putt, you should crouch down behind your ball like Betty Dimpleton is and read the green.

Reading the green is observing the ground to see if there are any contours. Golf balls will always curve if the ground isn't level. In the picture, Bob Dimpleton noticed a hill in the green so he aimed to the left of the hole. Then the ball curved downhill and into the hole. Great putt BOB!!!

Bobby was tending the flag for his dad. This means the flag was in the hole before Bob putted and when his ball was rolling towards the hole, Bobby pulled the pin so the ball wouldn't hit it. Hitting the pin while putting on the green is a 2 stroke penalty. It's your choice to have someone tend the flag for you or pull it out before you putt.

-26-

The Dimpleton's Scorecard

After Betty's final putt, the Dimpleton's shook hands and thanked each other for the game. Then they went to the golf shop to get a drink and add up their scores. To Betty's surprise, she had her best score ever on a big course. Bob played great on the back nine but Bobby scored higher than he normally does. Check out their scorecard.

	1	2	3	4	5	6	7	8	9	OUT		10	11	12	13	14	15	16	17	18	IN	Total
Blue tee yardage	195	385	532	402	410	145	381	520	432	3402		398	360	485	365	178	404	320	165	503	3178	6580
White tee yardage	180	365	519	369	386	123	345	500	397	3184		371	345	453	330	149	377	254	139	467	2885	6069
Hole #	1	2	3	4	5	6	7	8	9	OUT		10	11	12	13	14	15	16	17	18	IN	Total
Bob	3	4	6	4	4	5	4	4	4	38		3	4	3	4	3	3	4	2	4	30	68
Betty	4	5	4	4	3	2	4	4	5	35		4	5	5	4	4	4	4	3	4	37	72
Bobby	3	4	4	6	4	3	4	6	3	37		4	4	5	5	2	4	3	4	5	36	73
Par	3	4	5	4	4	3	4	5	4	36		4	4	5	4	3	4	4	3	5	36	72
Red tee yardage	167	315	443	315	337	107	308	440	355	2787		308	306	409	311	127	322	214	103	426	2526	5313

The Dimpleton Family

Good Luck with your golf!!!

Maybe one day we'll see you on the P.G.A or L.P.G.A. tour.

Now that you have finished reading Golf 101, Bob Dimpleton would like to see if you can answer the following questions:

1. How many birdies did Bob make on the Dimpleton's scorecard?

2. List the following clubs by how far they hit a golf ball, from shortest to farthest?   [ ] 9iron   [ ] 3wood   [ ] 5iron

3. Why is custom club fitting so important?

4. What does the finish position of a golf swing look like?

5. What is your 1st priority in golf ? (Circle 1)   Golf Swing   Safety   Rules

6. If your ball flies into the water, where are you allowed to drop a new ball, after adding 1 penalty stroke to your score?

7. Why should you fix your ball mark after your ball lands on the green?

8. Can you list the parts of a golf course?

9. Where should you avoid placing your golf equipment?

10. How do you read the green?

All answers are provided in the book.

My hope for you is that by reading and studying this book, you will gain the confidence to play all your rounds of golf in a fun and proper way.